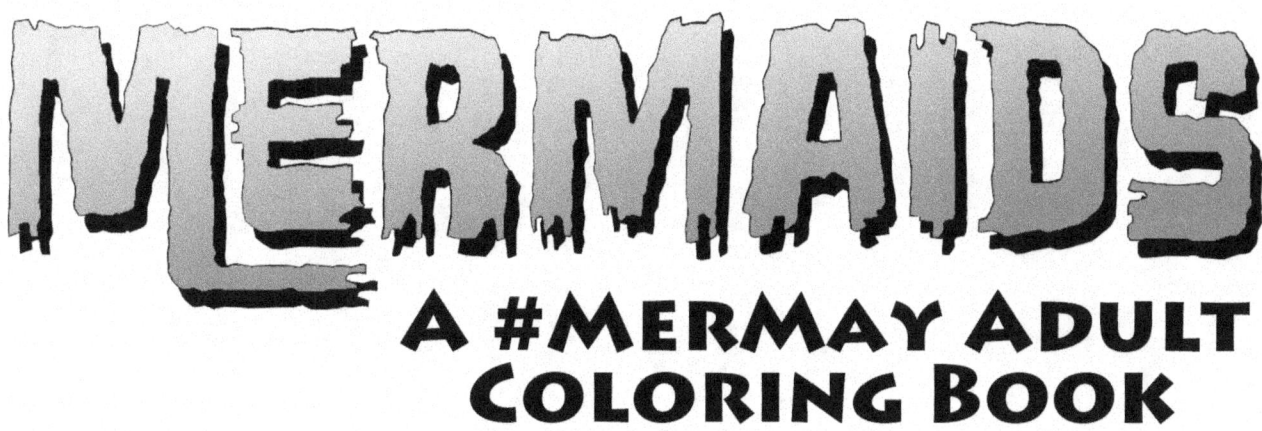

MERMAIDS
A #MerMay Adult Coloring Book

By Tom Bancroft (and YOU)

For more about or by TomBancroft:
TomBancroftstudio.com
Facebook: Facebook.com/bancroftbros
Twitter and Instagram: tombancroft1
Art instruction at taughtbyapro.com
and search my name on Amazon.com

ISBN:
ISBN-13: 978-1534965256
ISBN-10: 1534965254

Hello!

I'm Tom Bancroft, the artist behind the mermaid drawings you are about to color. I just want to say thank you for picking up this book and hope it provides you with lots of fun, challenges, and- most of all- a great distraction and form of relaxation for you. I've drawn my entire life (many decades now) and I still LOVE to draw everyday.

If you enjoy this coloring book, I hope to make many, many more with different subjects. This book is the first based on drawings I created in May of 2016 when I launched the hashtag #MerMay as a way to challenge myself and other artists around the world to draw everyday. Specifically, to draw a mermaid everyday in the month of May. I plan on bringing #MerMay back every year. If you are an artist on Instagram and other places, I hope you will join me next year!

In the meantime, enjoy coloring my artwork and please post your coloring and tag me online so I can see what amazing things you did!

Draw from the heart,
Tom Bancroft

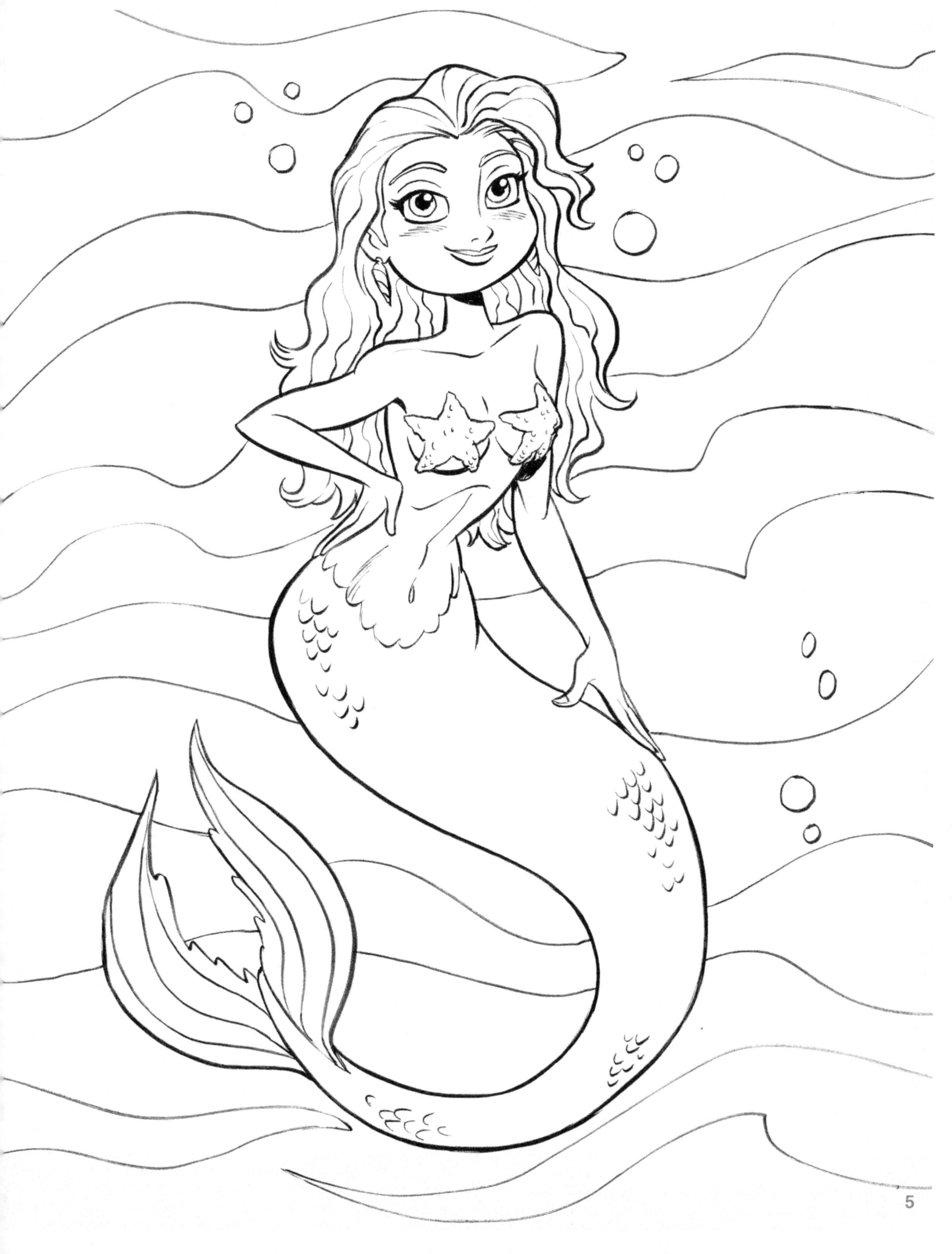

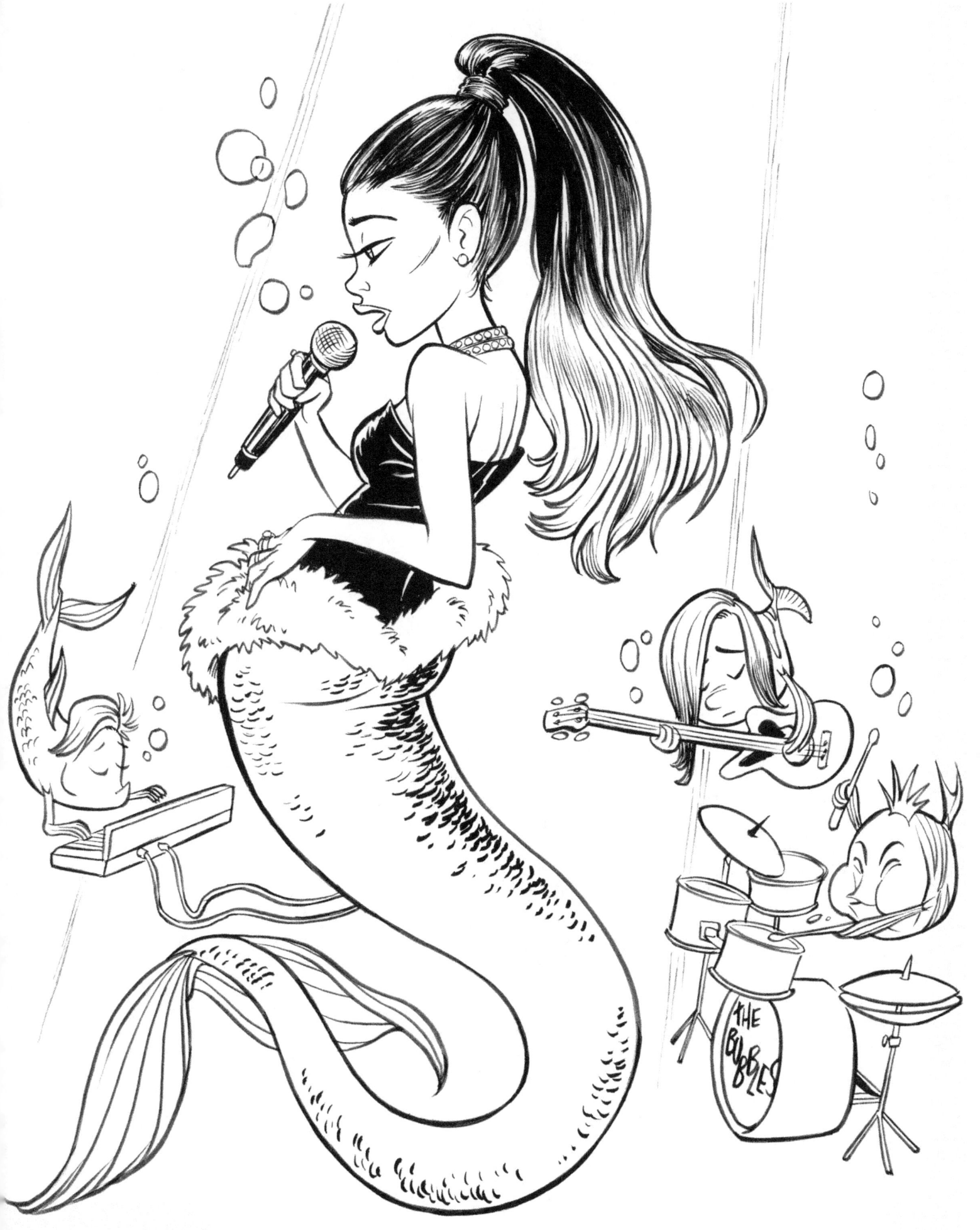

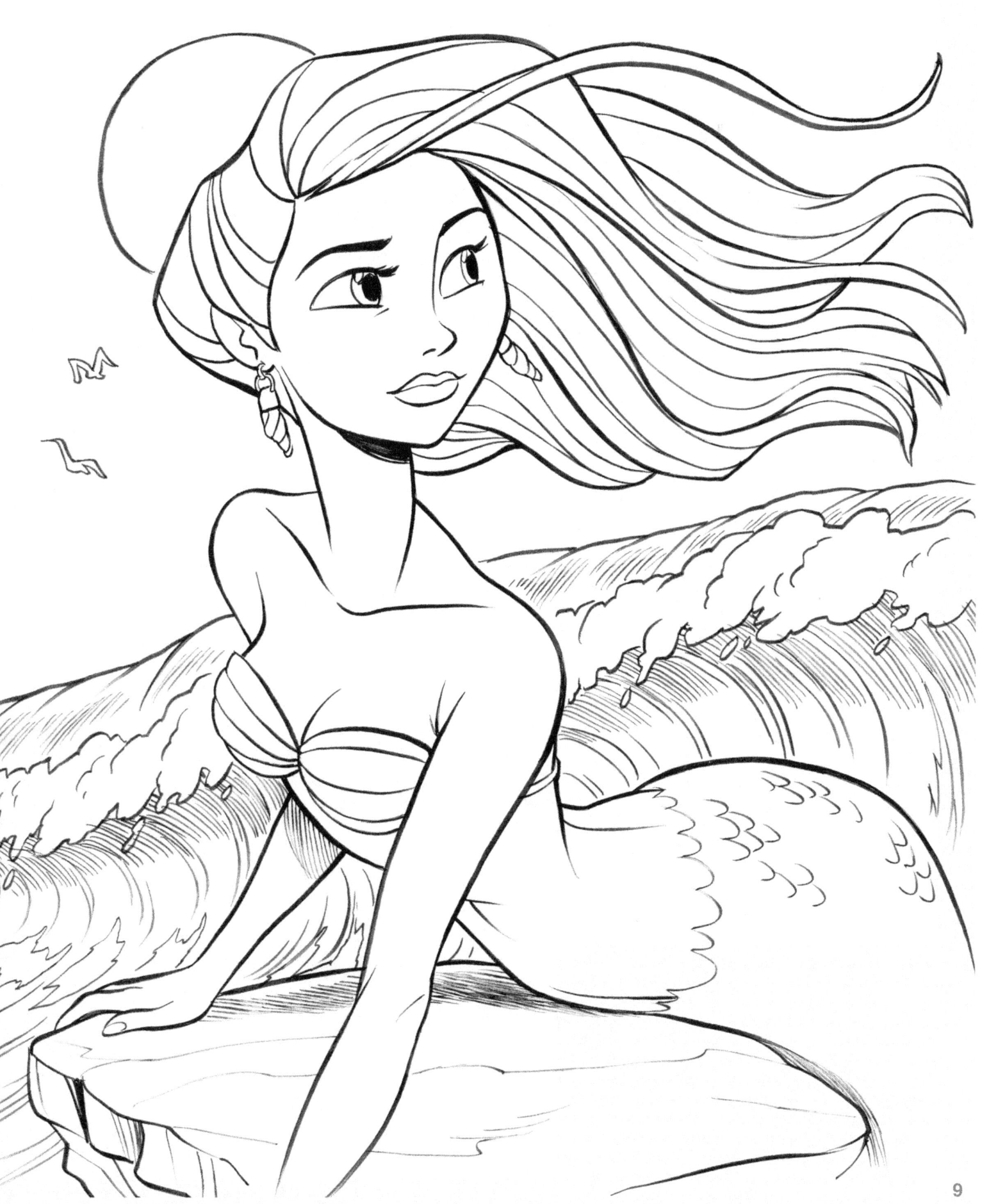

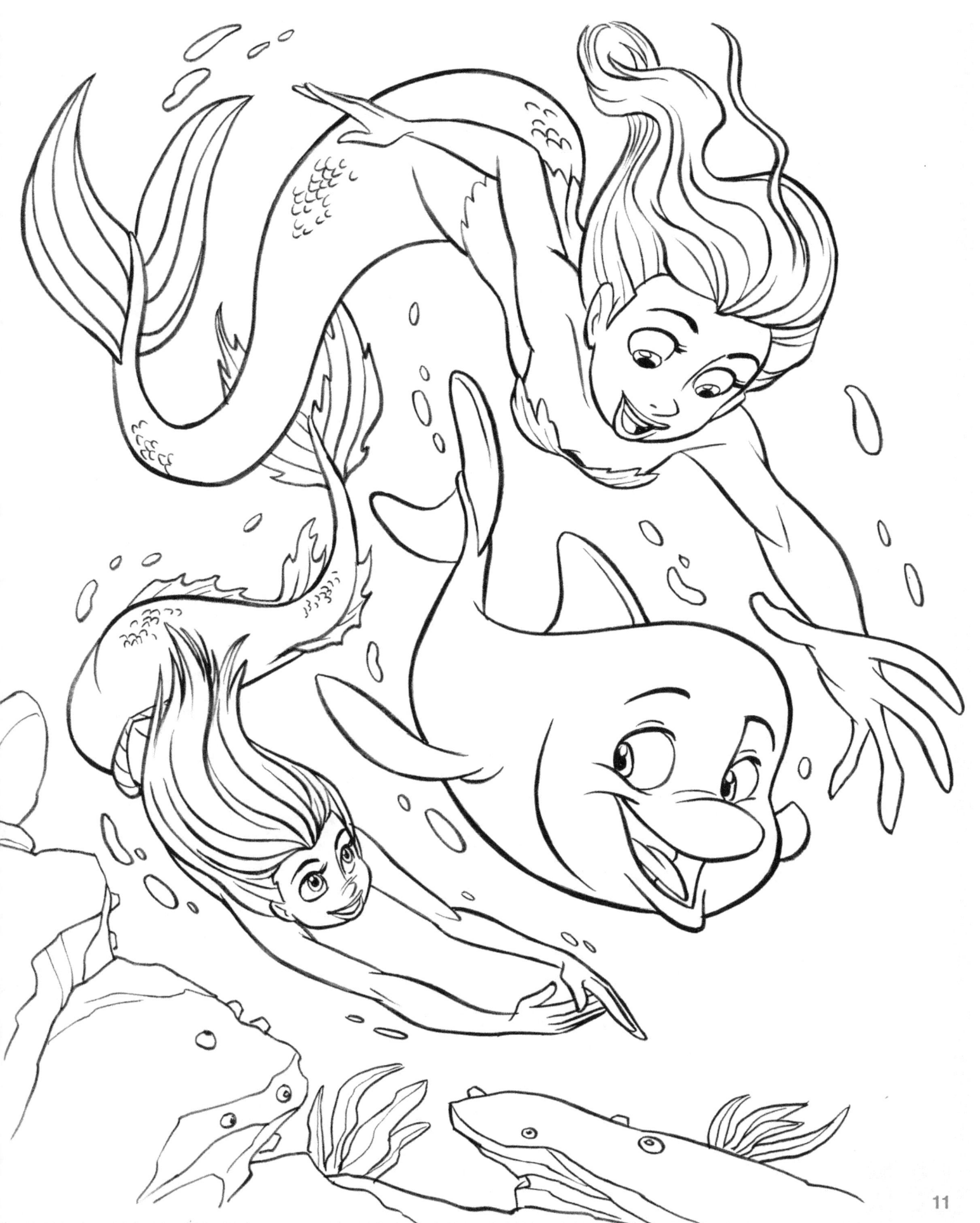

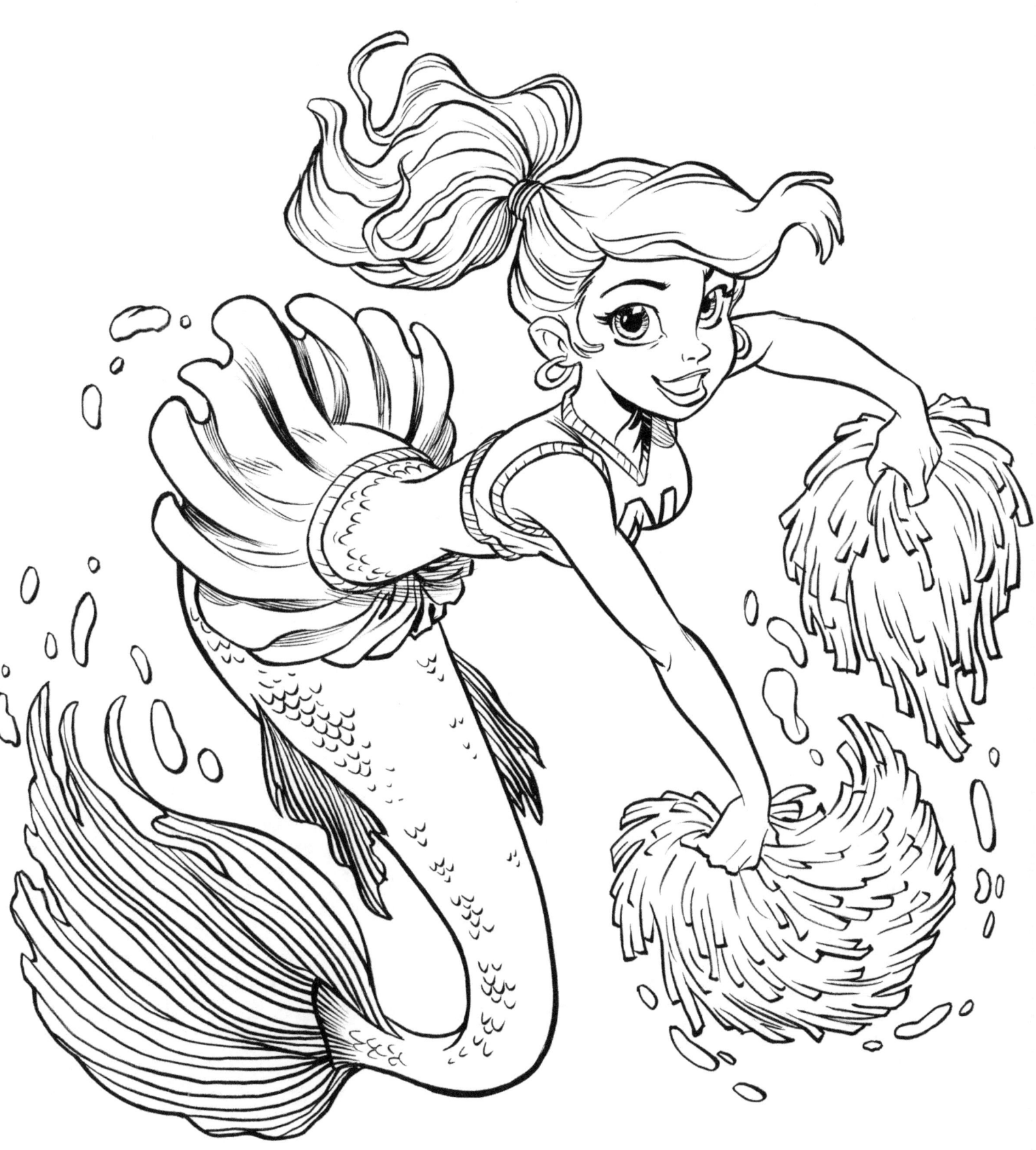

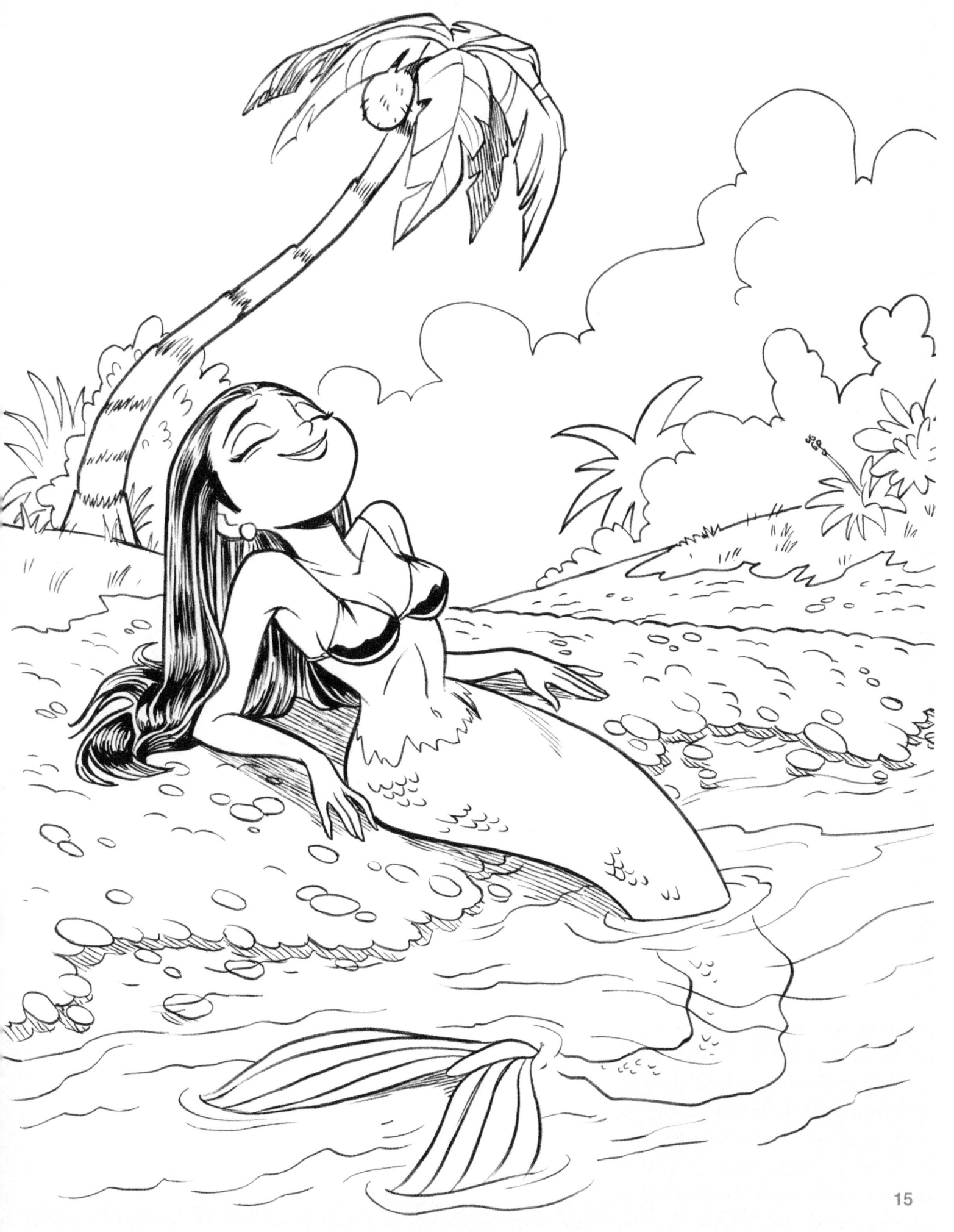

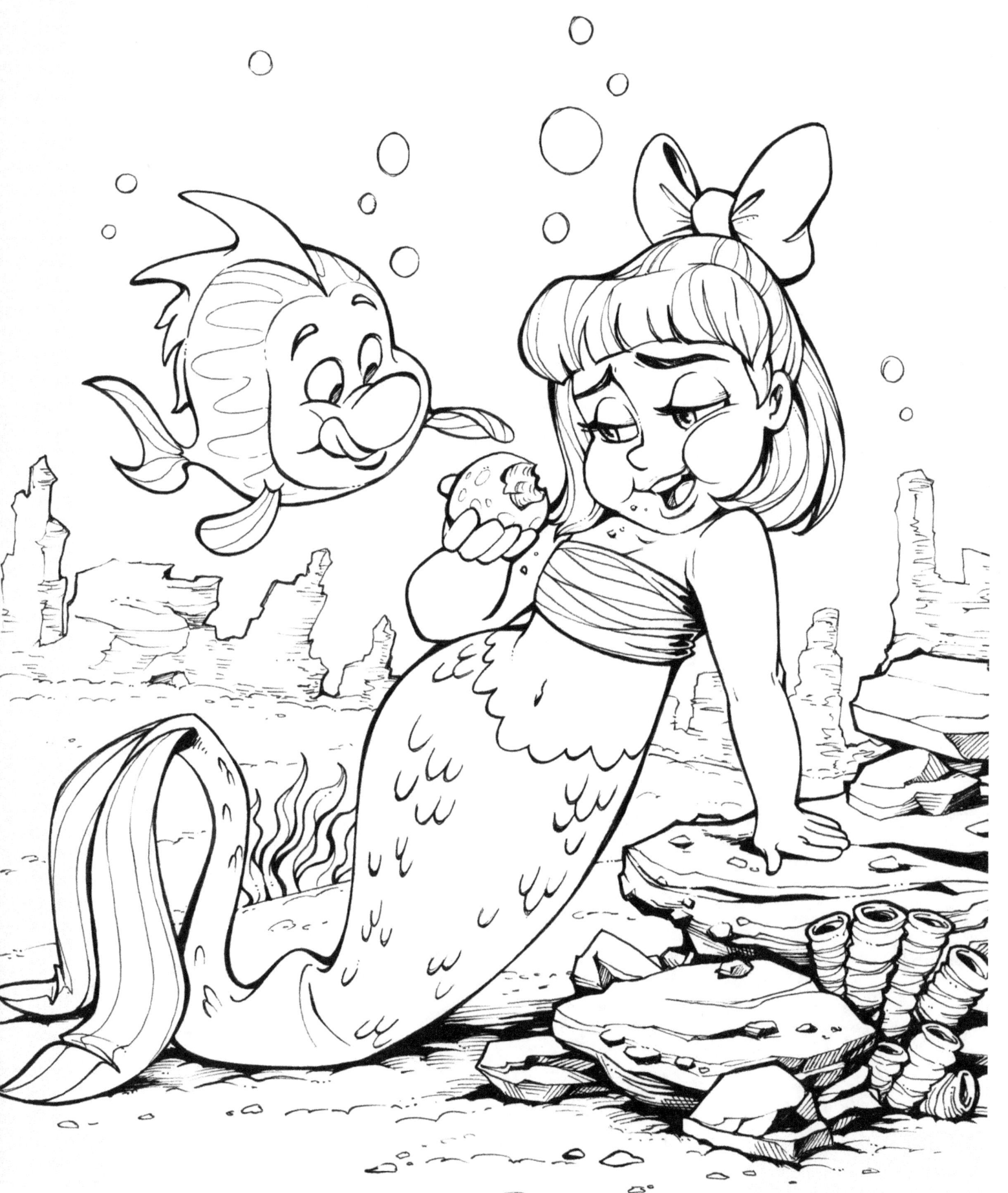

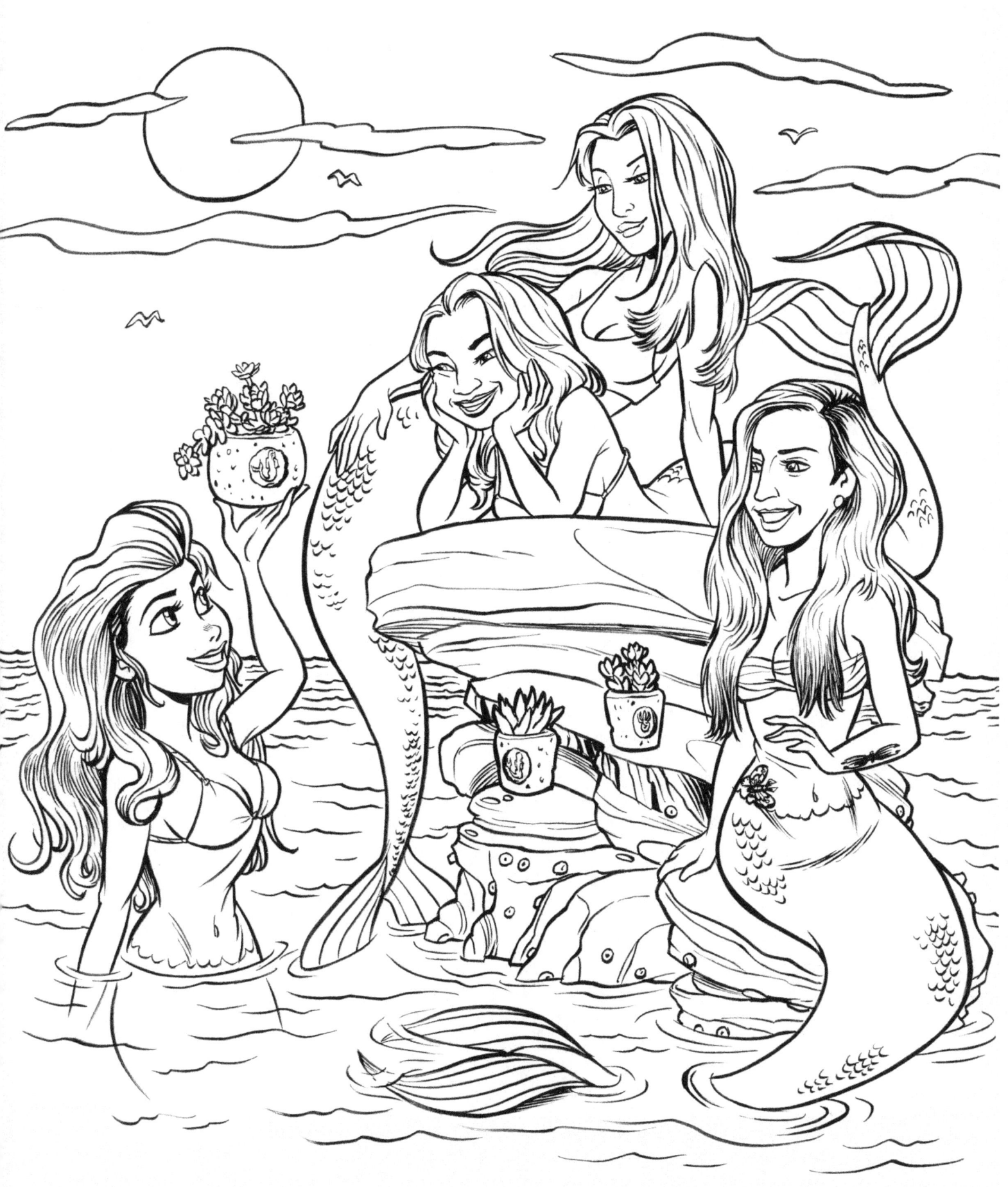

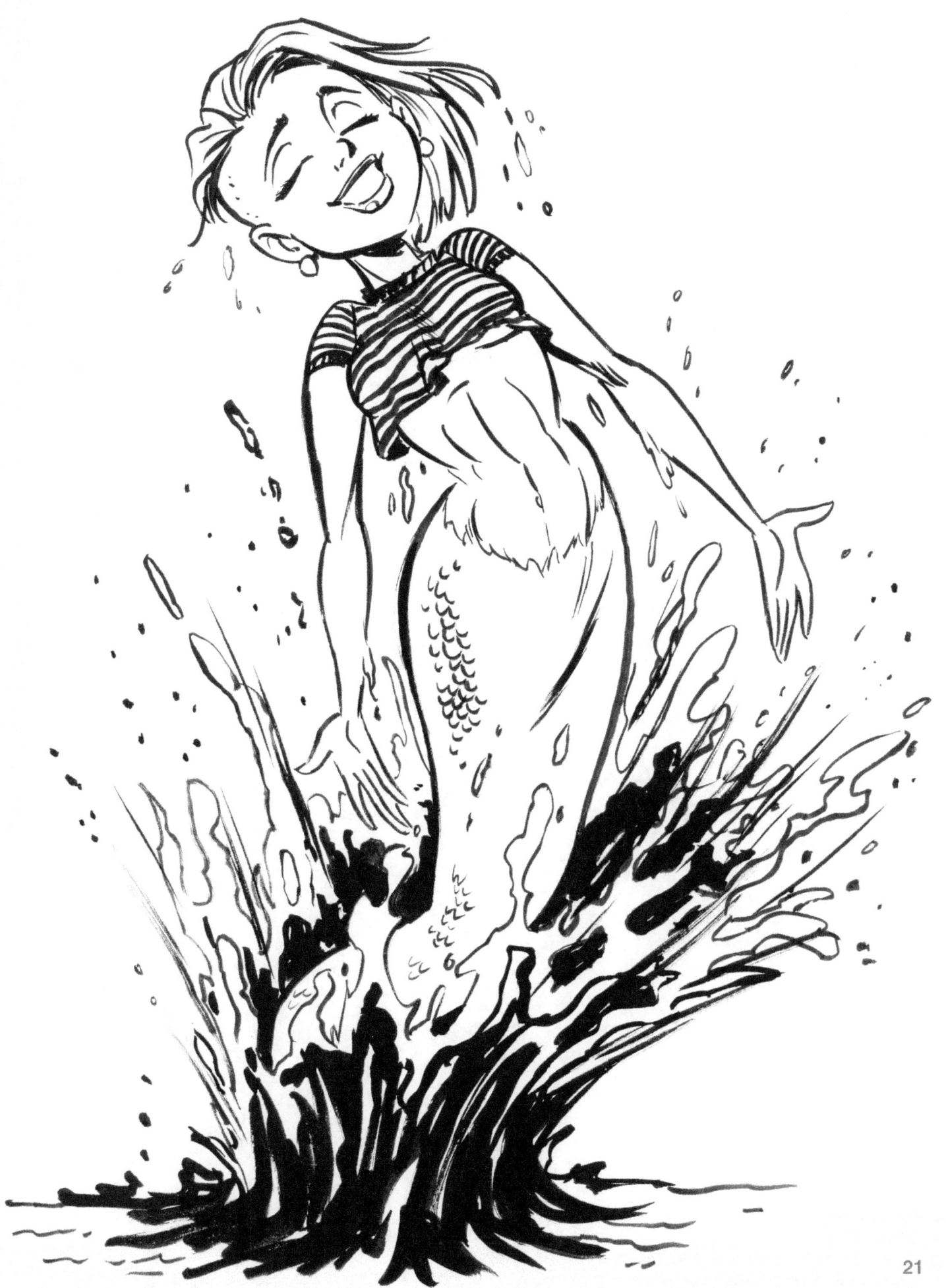

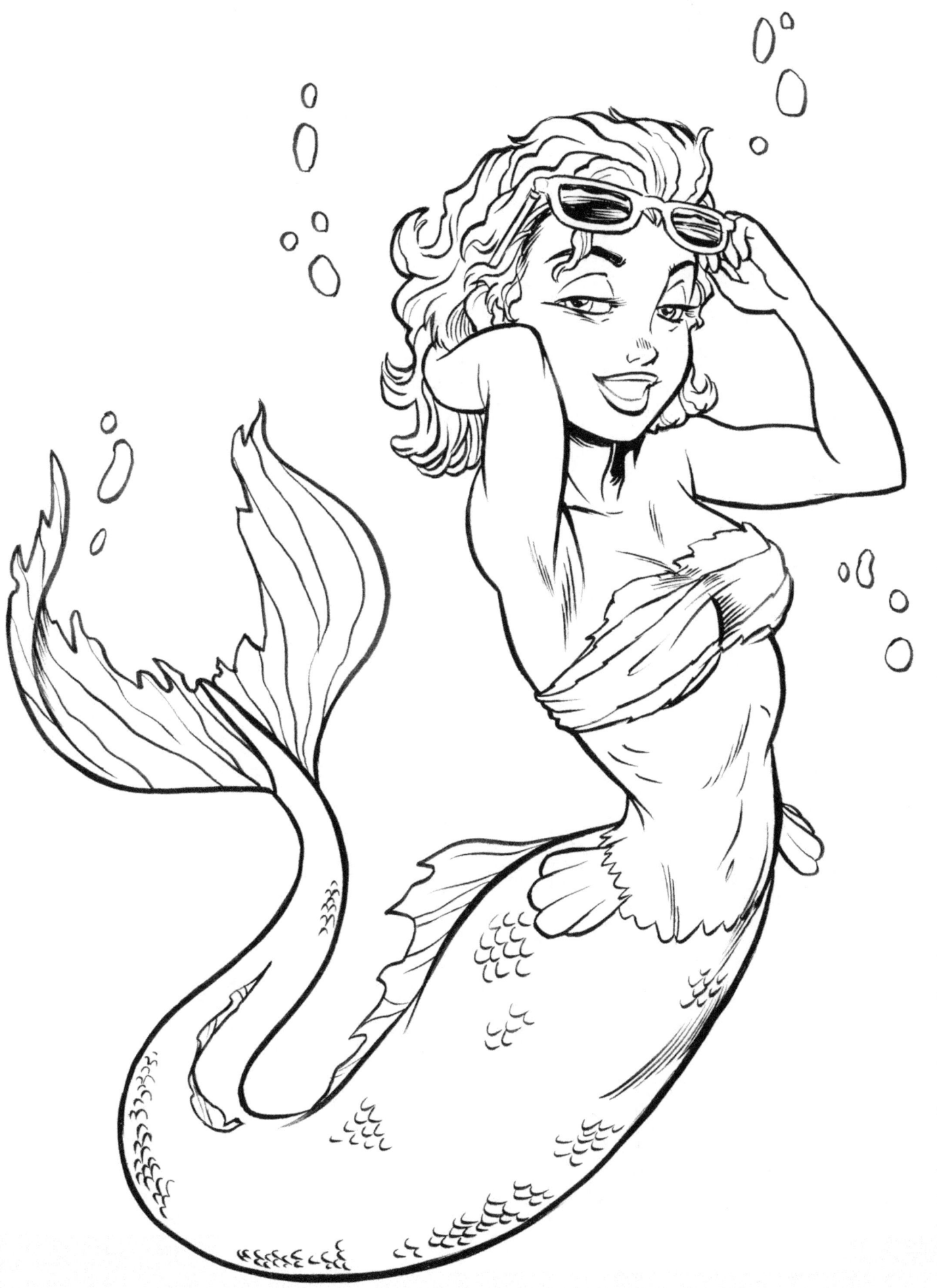

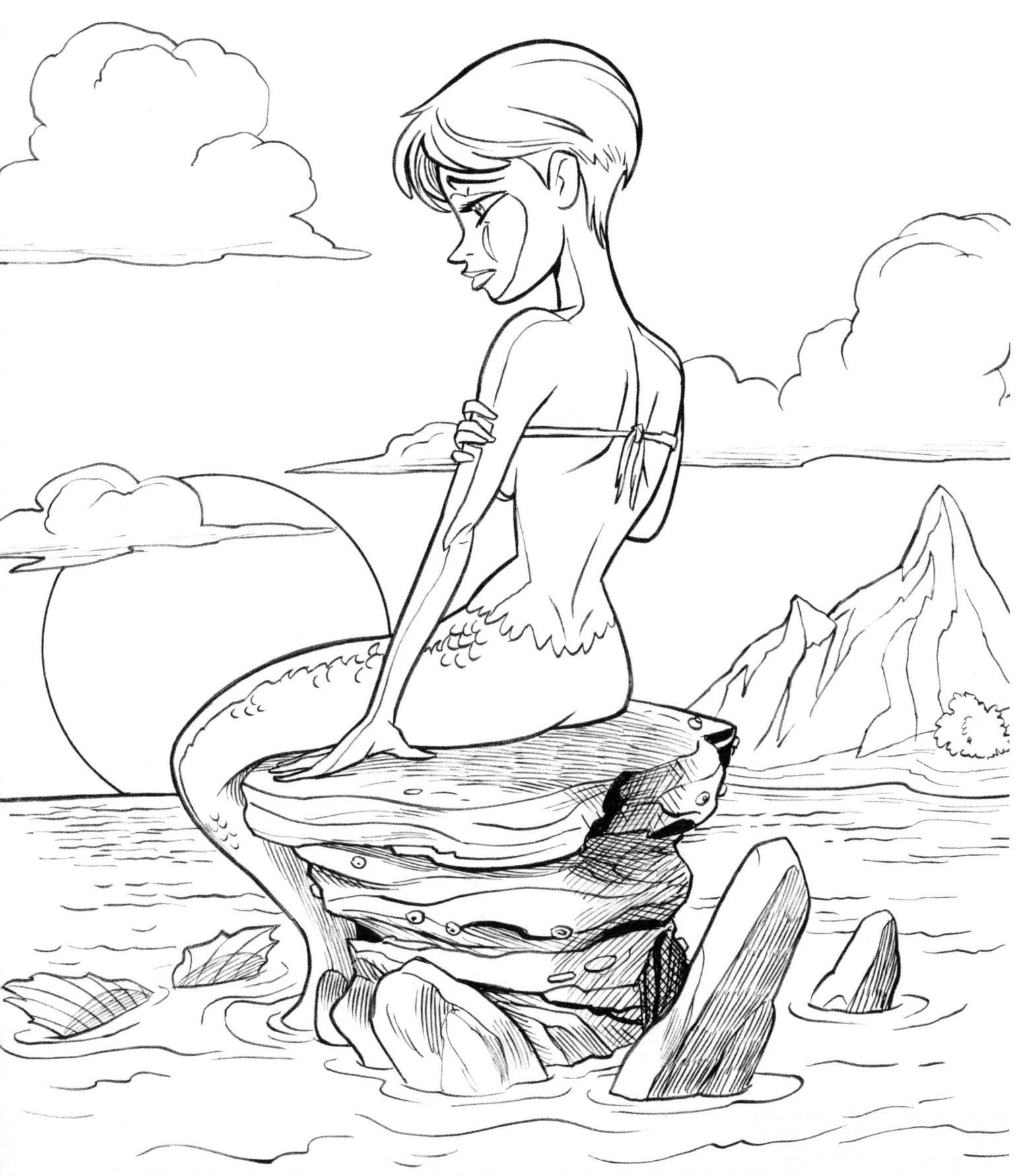

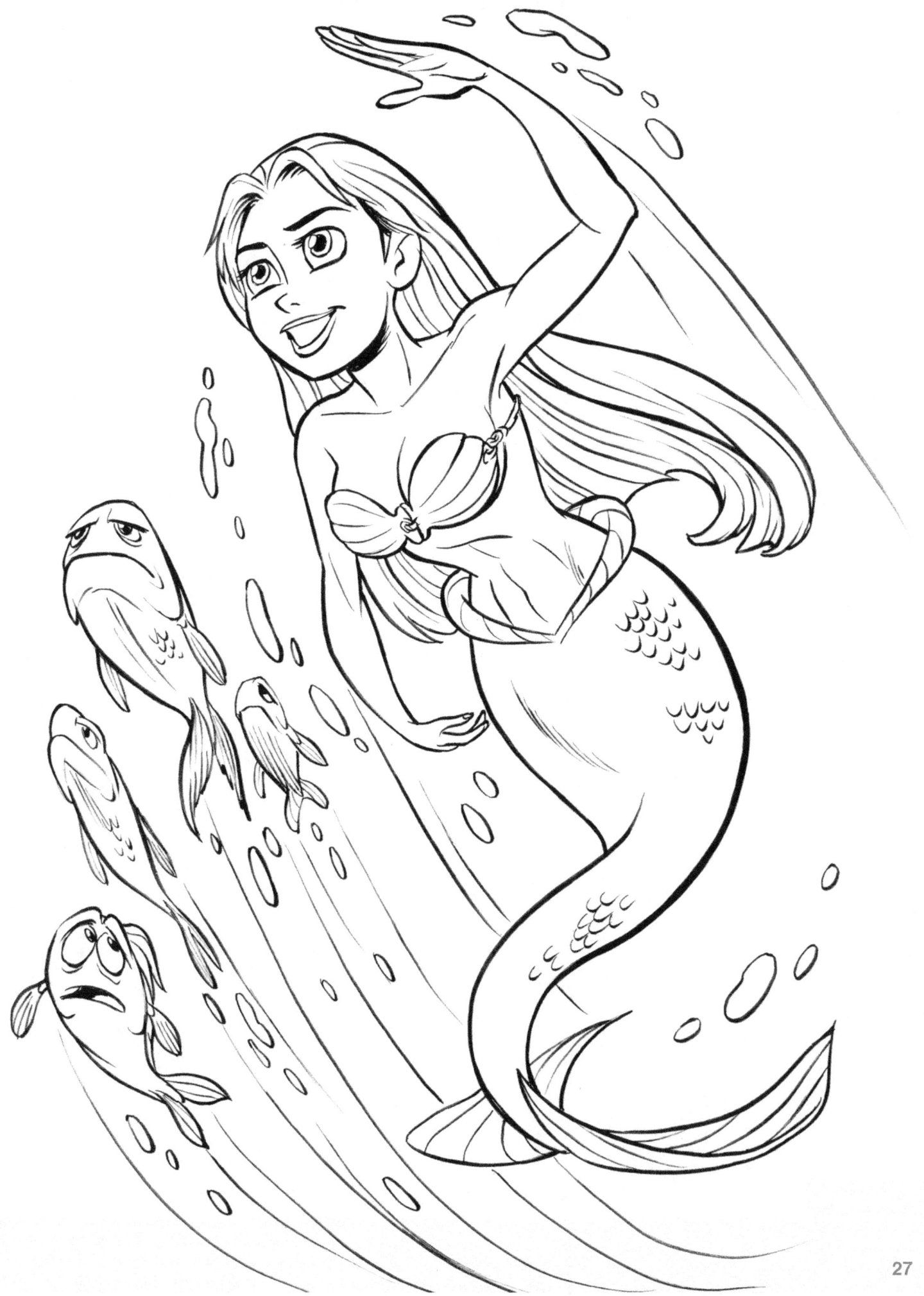

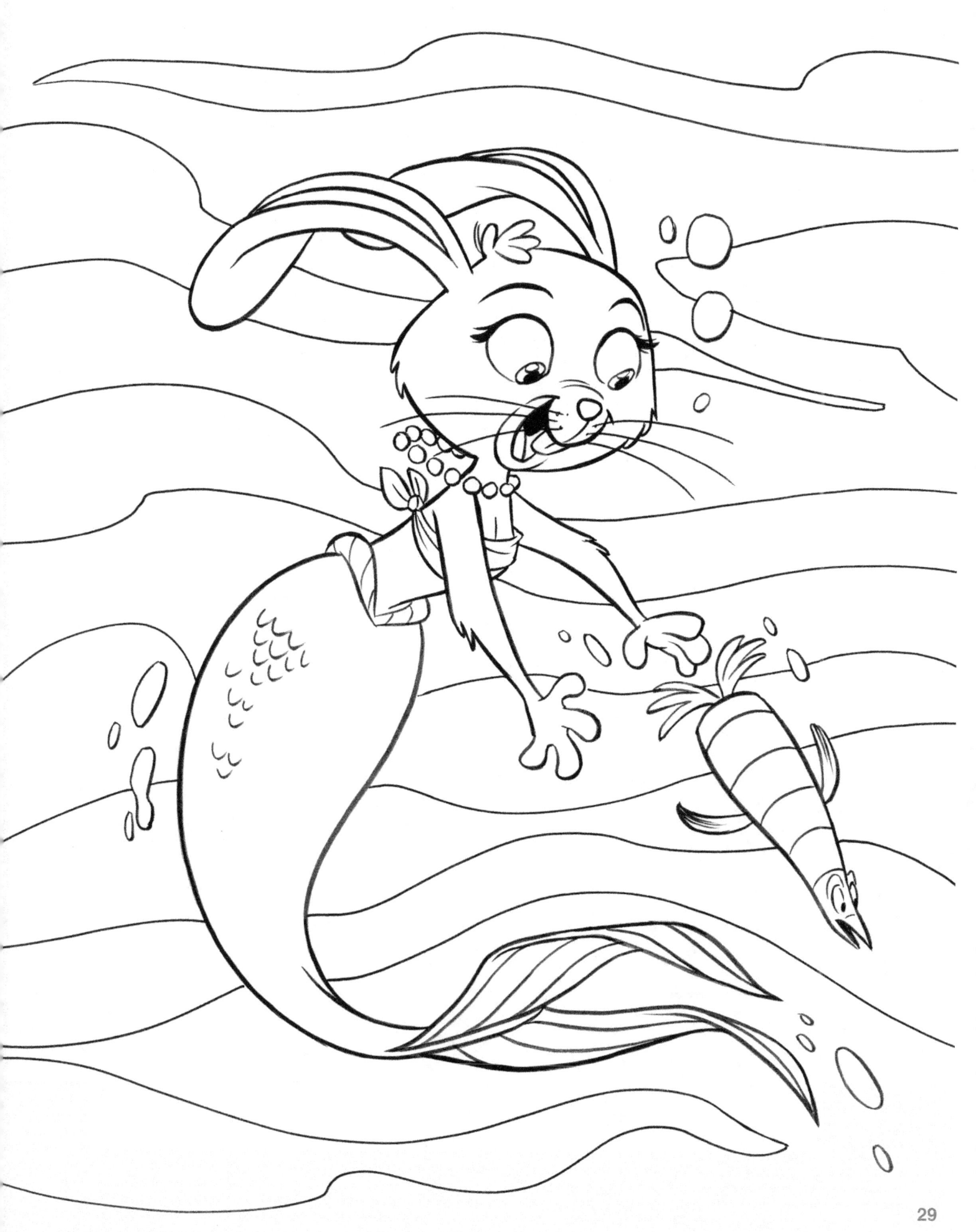

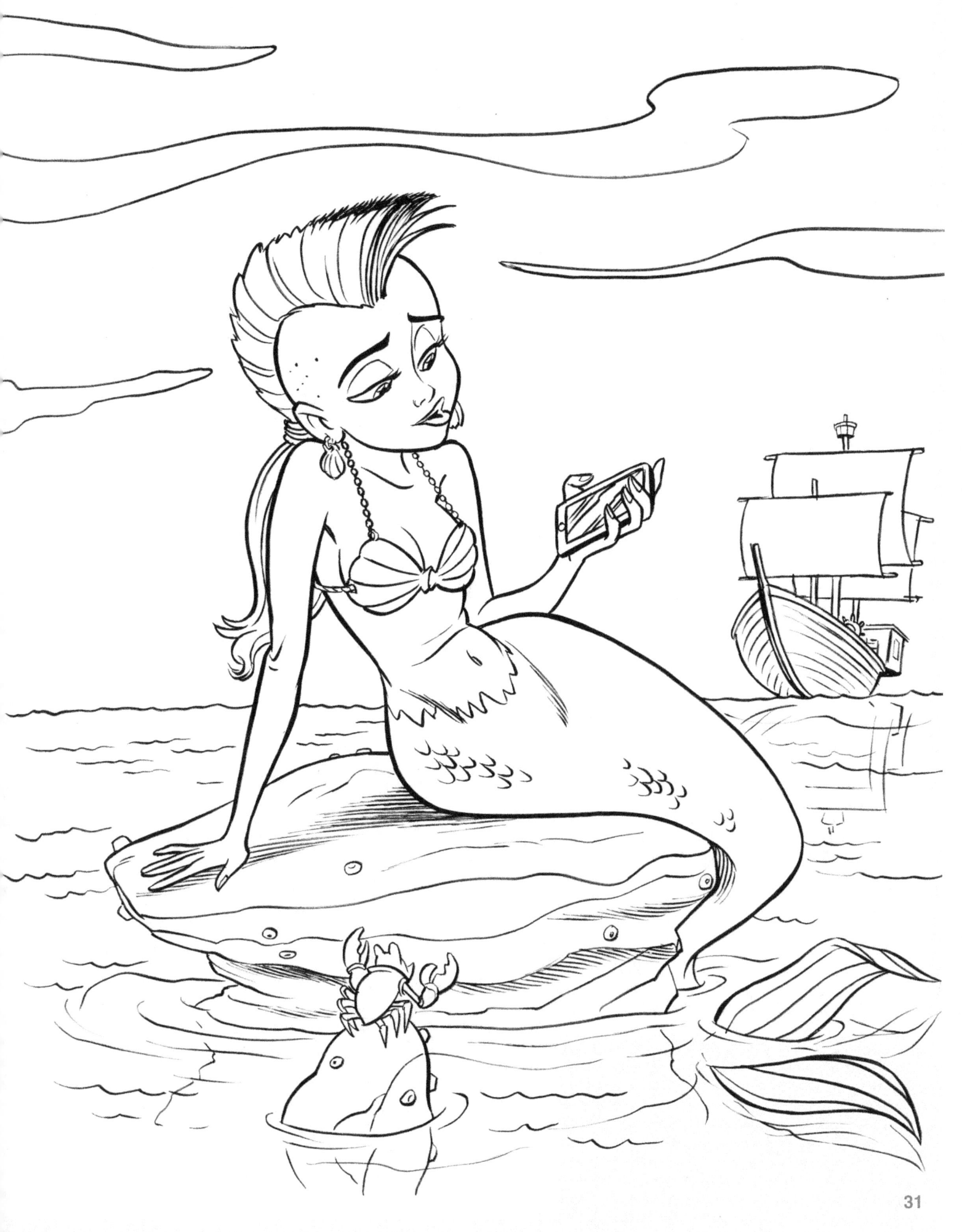

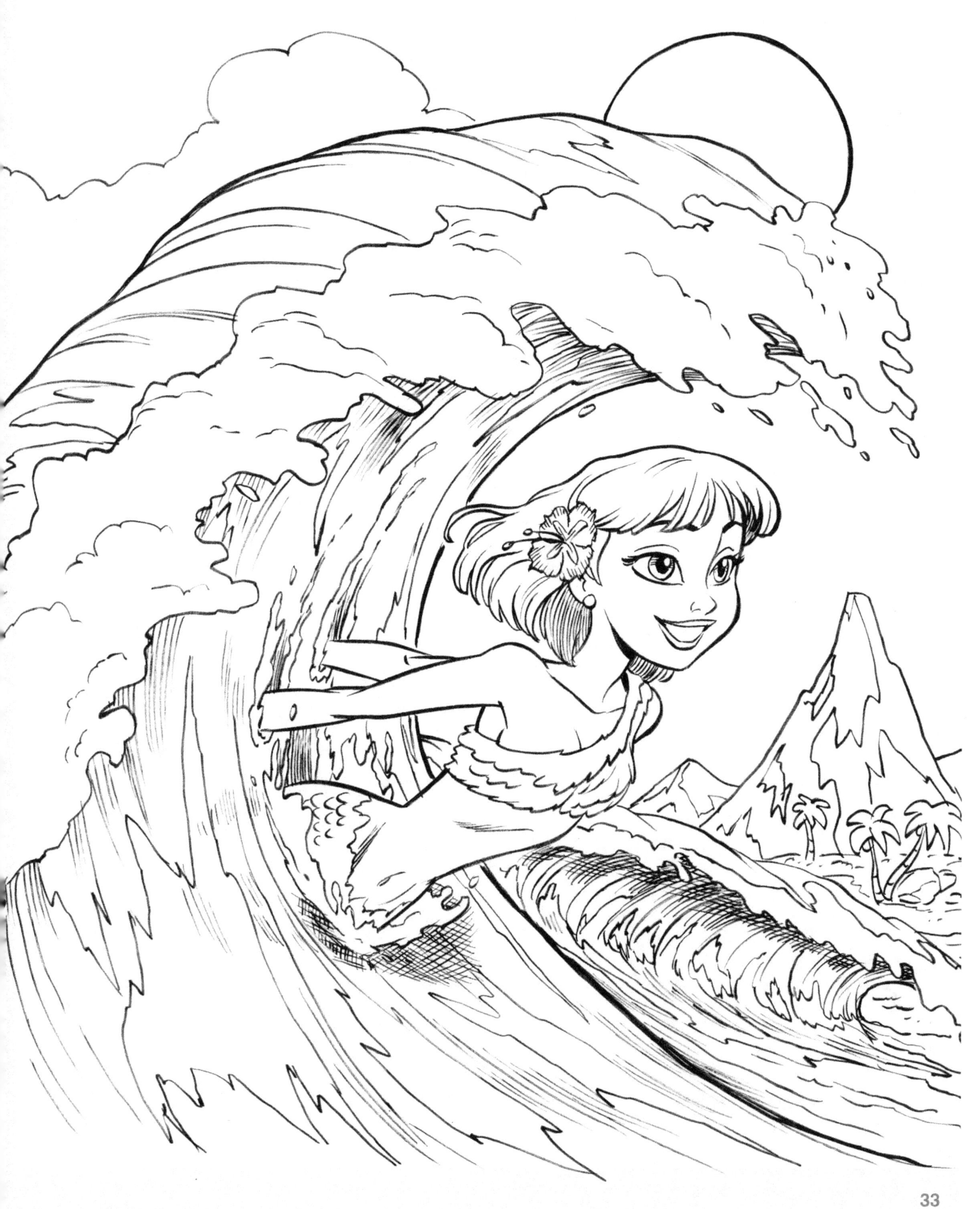

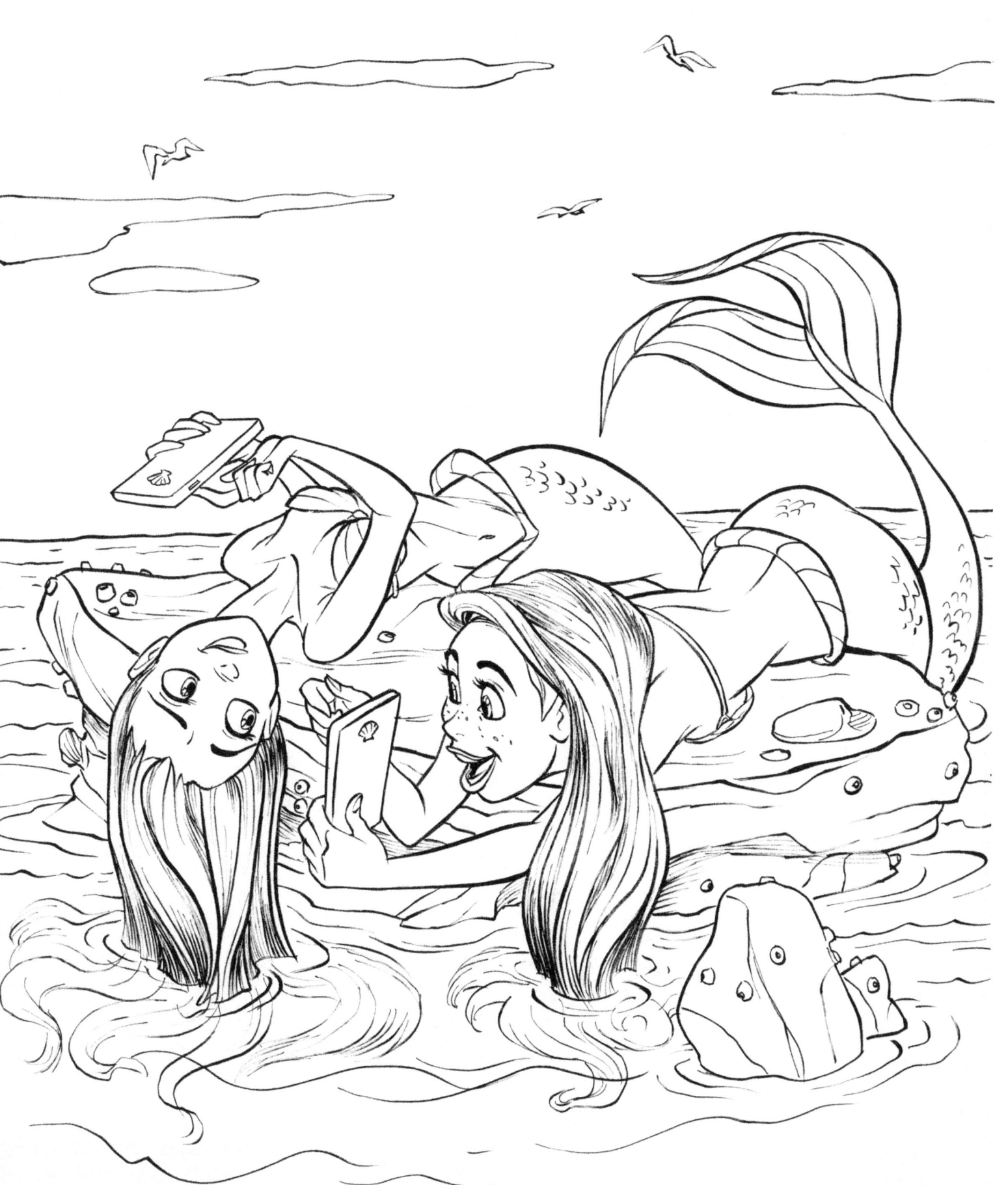

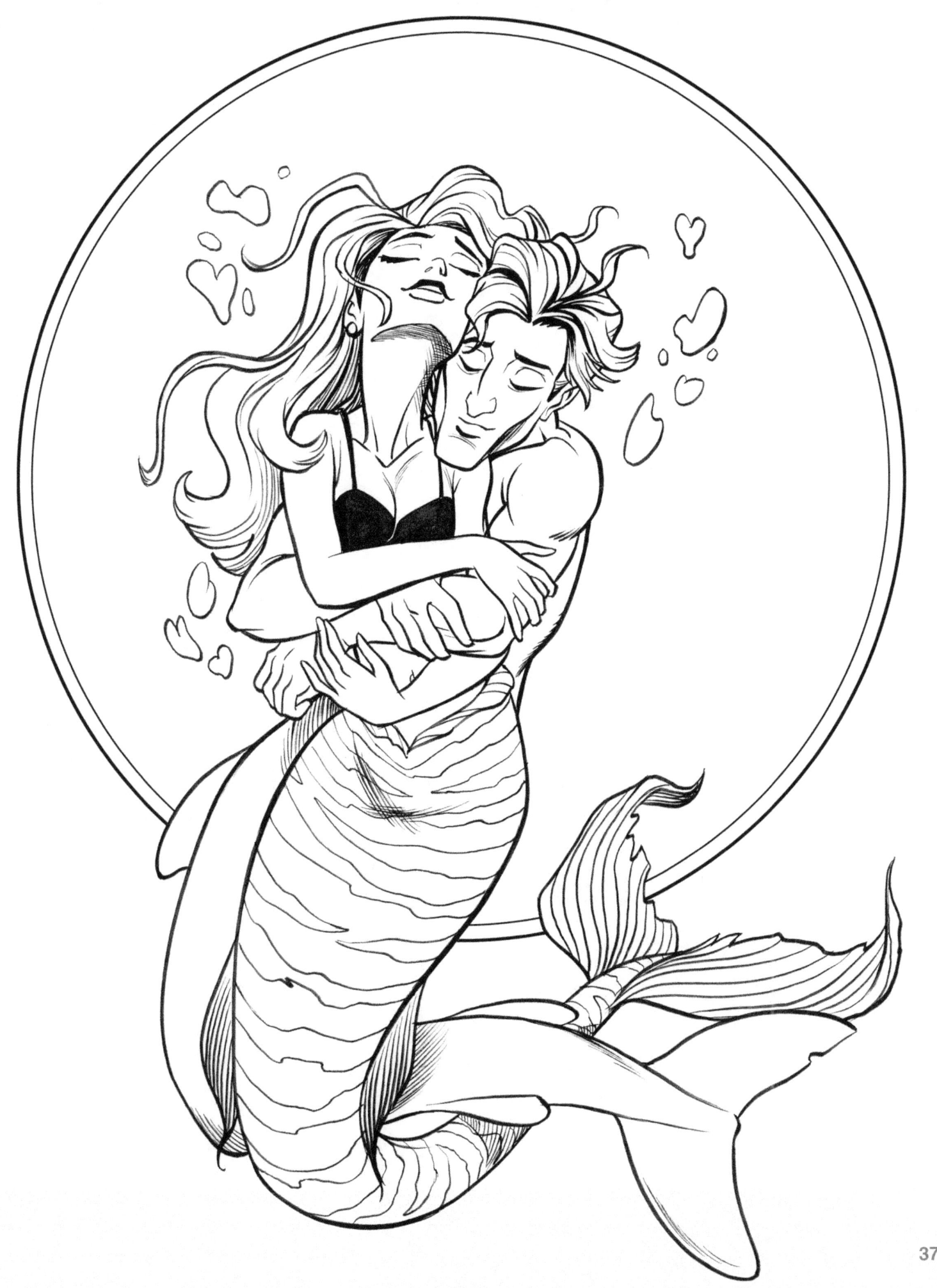

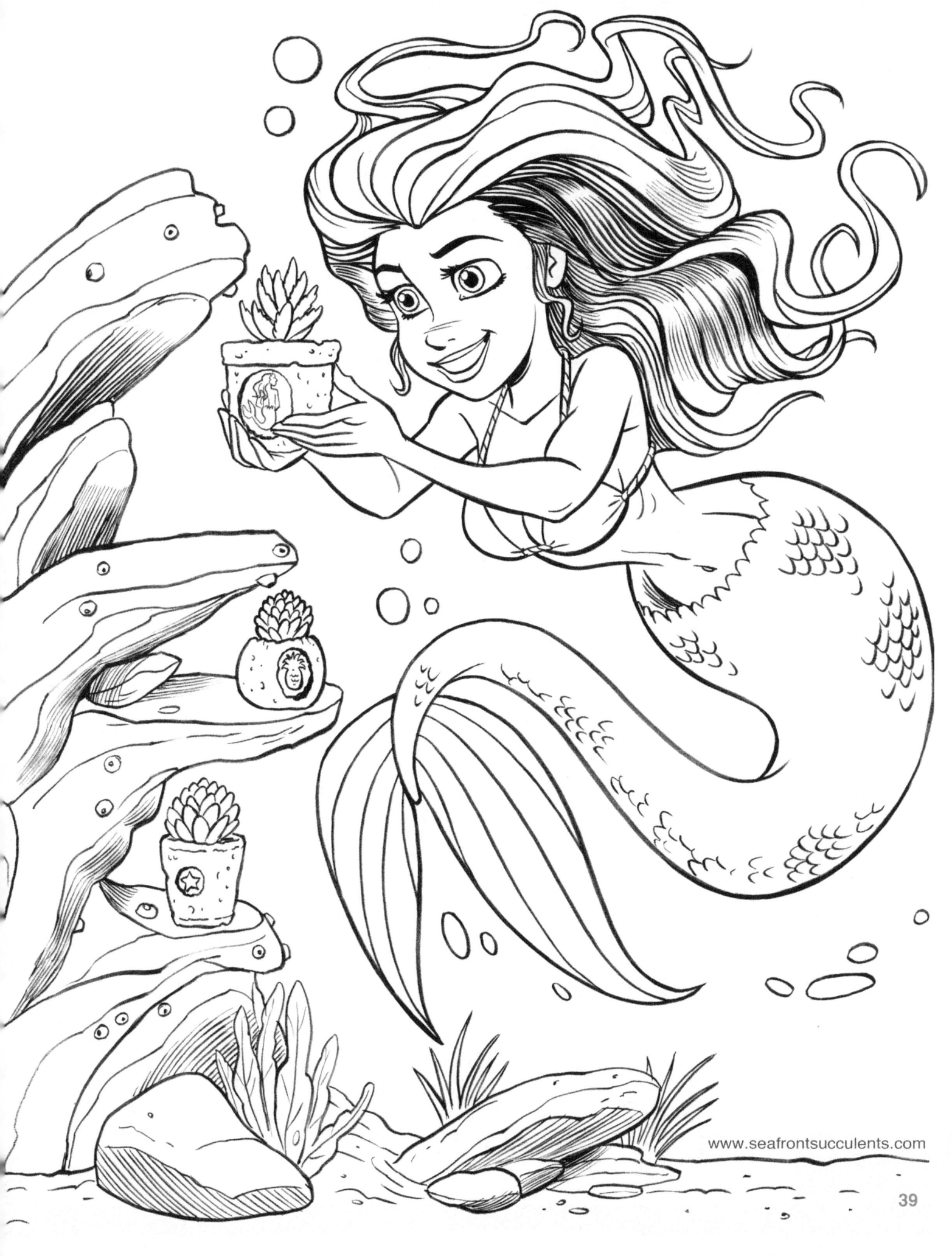

www.seafrontsucculents.com

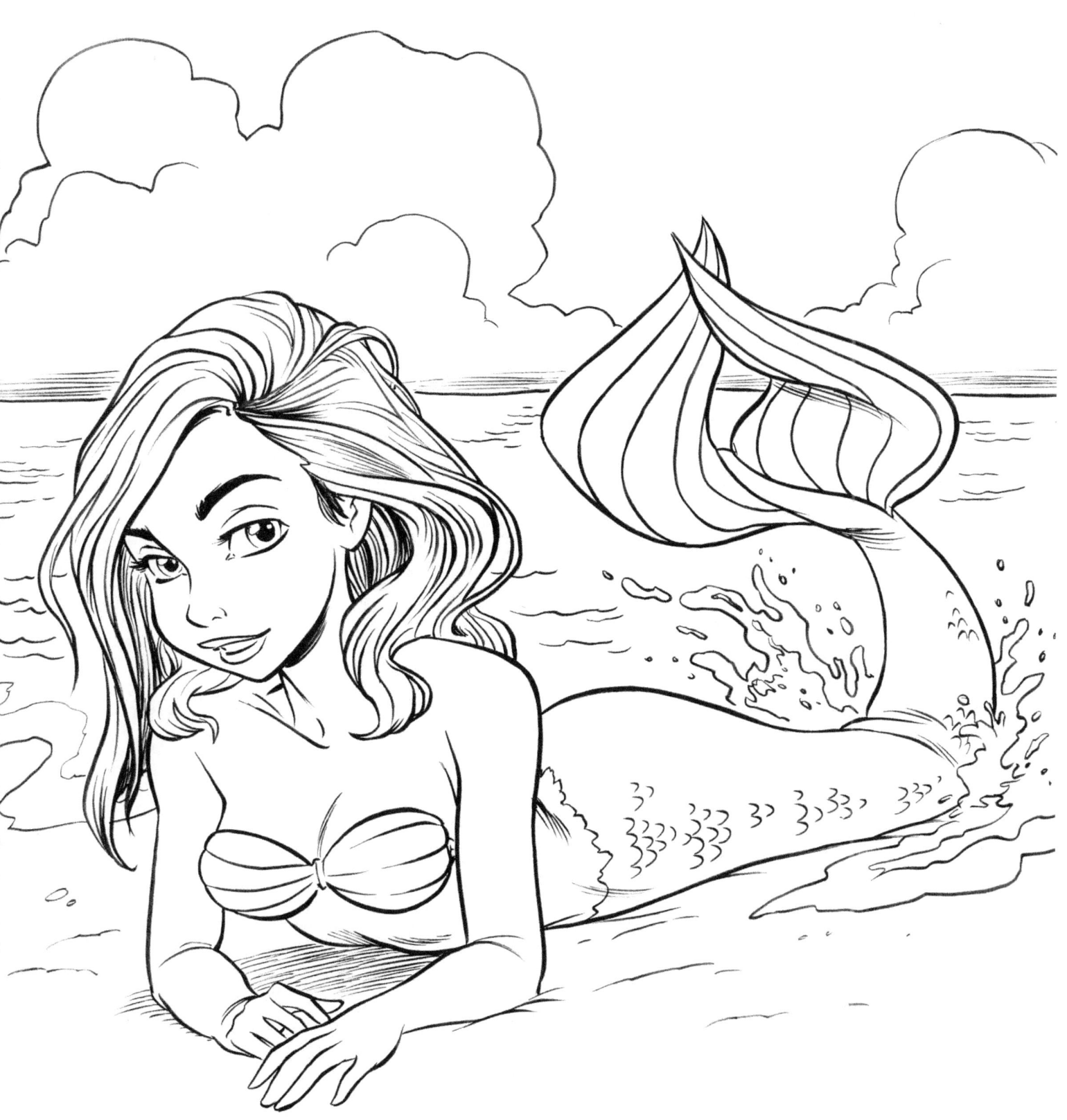

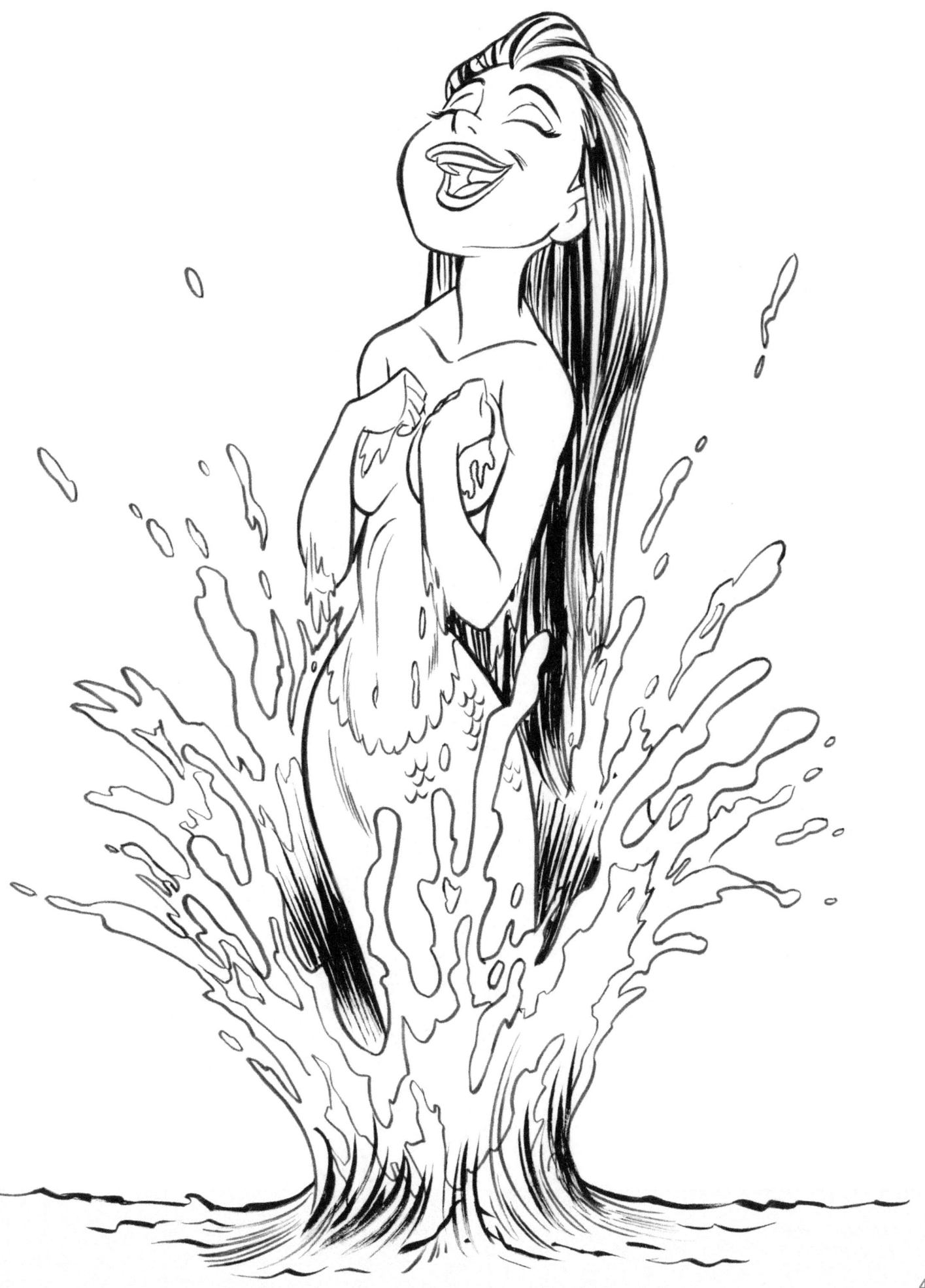

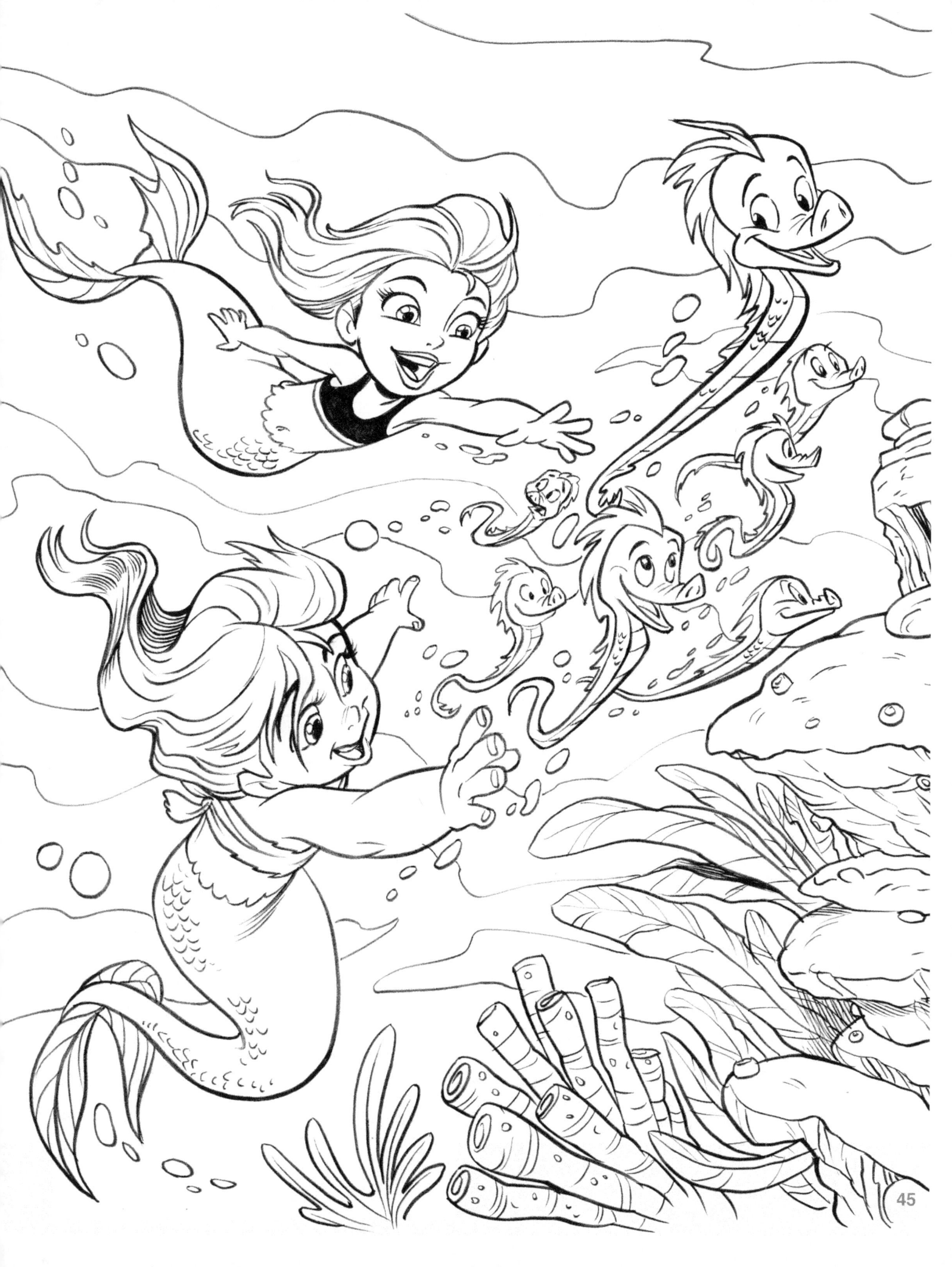

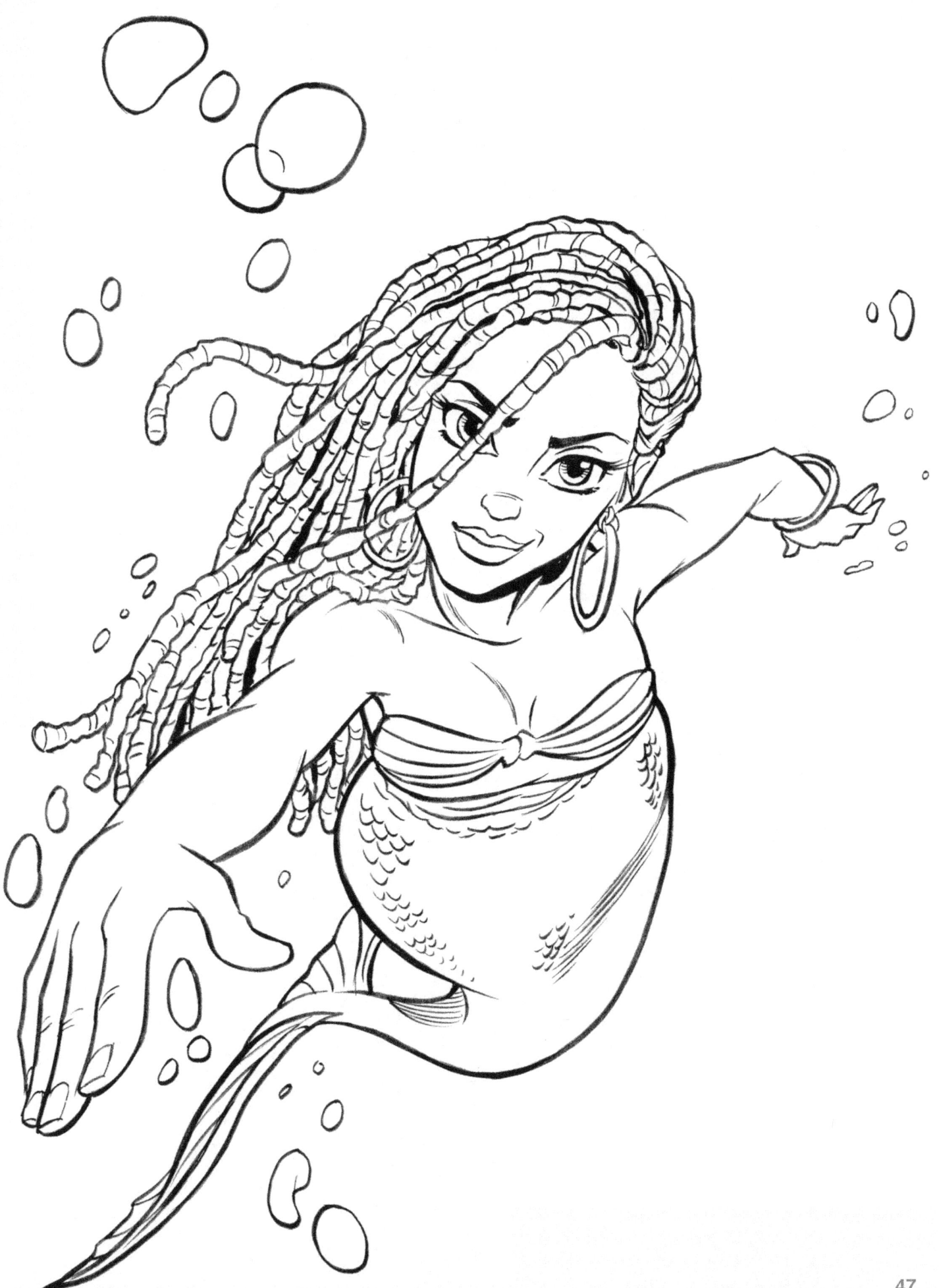